First Phrases from Around the World
Everyday Portuguese
Tricia Hoffman
Little Mitchie
an imprint of Mitchell Lane

CREATING YOUNG NONFICTION READERS

Little Mitchie books spark curiosity and support early nonfiction reading for students in Grades 2-3. Designed to build vocabulary, support second language learners, and prepare readers for middle-grade content, each book includes helpful tips for parents and educators to build confidence and deepen understanding of the world.

TIPS FOR READING NONFICTION WITH BEGINNING READERS

Talk about Nonfiction

Begin by explaining that nonfiction books give us information that is true. The book will be organized around a specific topic or idea, and we may learn new facts through reading.

Look at the Parts

Most nonfiction books have helpful features. Our *Little Mitchie* titles include color photographs and graphic aids, a table of contents, a glossary, and an index. Share the purpose of these features with your reader.

Color Photos and Graphic Aids

A lot of information can be found by "reading" photos, charts, maps, and other graphic aids found within nonfiction texts. Help your reader learn more about the different ways information can be displayed.

Table of Contents

Located at the front of the book, this list shows the big ideas within the text and the page numbers where they can be found.

Index

Located at the back of the book, an index is an alphabetical list of topics and the page numbers where they can be found.

With a little help and guidance about reading nonfiction, you can feel good about introducing a young reader to the world of *Little Mitchie* nonfiction books.

Little Mitchie is an imprint of:

Mitchell Lane
PUBLISHERS

2001 SW 31st Avenue
Hallandale, FL 33009
mitchelllanepub.com

First Edition, 2027.

Author: Tricia Hoffman
Designer: Kathy Walsh
Editor: Tricia Hoffman

Library of Congress Cataloging-in-Publication Data
Title: Everyday Portuguese / by Tricia Hoffman

Description: Hallandale, FL :
Mitchell Lane Publishers, [2027]

Identifiers:
Library bound ISBN: 979-8-89260-912-8
Paperback ISBN: 979-8-90145-063-5
eBook ISBN: 979-8-90145-022-2

Library of Congress Control Number: 2026930177

PHOTO CREDITS: Cover and Title pg: iukhym_vova, smile3377; Doodle Art: devitaayu, FourLeafLover, wanchana, veekicl, Rizky, mhatzapa, Kebon doodle, Asyam Design, piixypeach, syoko: istock: background, rica nohara; p 4, Bricolage, Andrey Arkusha, Prostock-studio; p 5, antoniodiaz; p 6, Gelpi, Krakenimages.com, fizkes; p 7, Eric Isselee, AYO Production; p 9, New Africa; p 10, PeopleImages, India Picture, Family Stock; p 11, Roman Samborskyi; p 12, Chiociolla, Chase D'animulls, BongoStock, Rido; p 13, Bet_Noire, Sorapop Udomsri, Roman Samborskyi; p 14, Ground Picture, Miljan Zivkovic, Prostock-Studio; p 15, Poltu Shyamal, New Africa; p 16, Ground Picture, Lopolo, Ljupco Smokovski; p 17, KPG-Payless; p 18, Pixel-Shot, Ljupco Smokovski, Volodymyr TVERDOKHLIB; p 19, adriaticfoto, gothiclolita; p20 Krakenimages.com, Marcos Castillo; p 21, Alexander Prokopenko, Krakenimages.com, StoryTime Studio, C-R-V, Mei Lan Photo; p 22, Amelia Fox, Prostock-studio, SofikoS, Pixel-Shot

Table of Contents

This Is Me

Eu tenho oito anos de idade.

I am eight years old.

Meu nome é João.

My name is João.

Este sou eu

um
one
dois
two
três
three
quatro
four
cinco
five
seis
six
sete
seven
oito
eight
nove
nine
dez
ten
Adeus!
Goodbye!

People and Pets

Pessoas e animais de estimação

Today

Hoje é quinta-feira.

Today is Thursday.

domingo
Sunday

segunda-feira
Monday

terça-feira
Tuesday

quarta-feira
Wednesday

quinta-feira
Thursday

sexta-feira
Friday

sábado
Saturday

O mês é fevereiro.

The month is February.

janeiro . . . . January
fevereiro . . . . . February
março . . . . March
abril . . . . April
maio . . . . May
junho . . . . June
julho . . . . July
agosto . . . . August
setembro . . . . September
outubro . . . . . . October
novembro . . . . November
dezembro . . . . December

Hoje

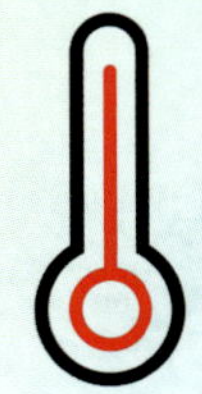

quente
hot

frio
cold

chuvoso
rainy

ventoso
windy

Morning

Eu penteio meu cabelo.

I comb my hair.

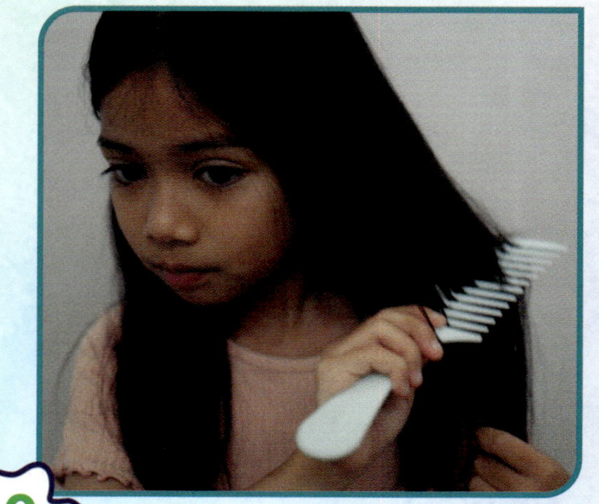

Eu escovo meus dentes.

I brush my teeth.

Manhã

Eu uso shorts azuis.

I wear blue shorts.

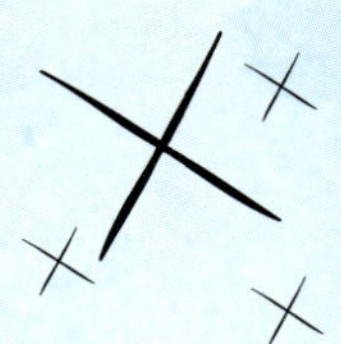

laranja	amarelo	azul	verde	
orange	yellow	blue	green	
roxo	vermelho	rosa	preto	branco
purple	red	pink	black	white

Breakfast

Quero cereal no café da manhã, por favor.

I want cereal for breakfast, please.

torrada
toast

suco de laranja
orange juice

bacon
bacon

ovo
egg

Café da manhã

O ônibus chegou.
É hora de ir!

The bus is here.
It is time to go!

ônibus escolar
school bus

mochila
backpack

School

Vou para a escola.

I go to school.

Eu leio.

I read.

Eu faço matemática.

I do math.

Escola

Preciso de ajuda.
I need help.

professora
teacher

mesa
desk

Posso ir ao banheiro?
May I go to the bathroom?

Time to Play

Você quer brincar comigo?
Will you play with me?
Sim!
Yes!
Eu corro.
I run.
Eu balanço.
I swing.

Hora de brincar

Neighborhood

Aceno para o meu amigo.

I wave to my friend.

Eu vou à loja.

I go to the store.

Vizinhança

Quanto custa isso?
How much does this cost?

árvore
tree

flores
flowers

calçada
sidewalk

grama
grass

Dinner

Sim, por favor.
Yes, please.

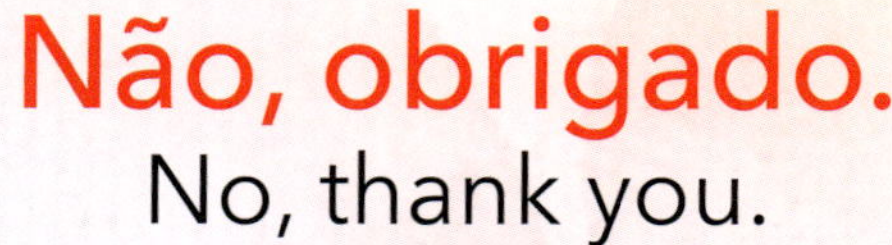

Não, obrigado.
No, thank you.

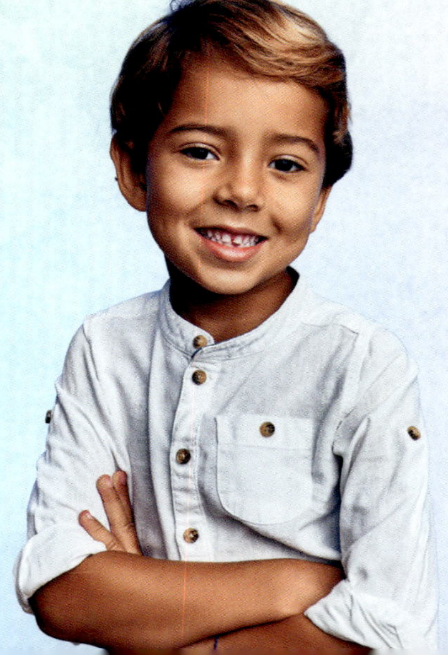

Jantar

Eu gosto de comida portuguesa.

I like Portuguese food.

caldo verde
soup

bifana
pork sandwich

arroz doce
rice pudding

Eu gosto de comida americana.

I like American food.

pizza
pizza

Night

Eu uso pijama.

I wear pajamas.

Eu vou para a cama.

I go to bed.

Eu fecho os olhos.

I close my eyes.

Noite

Boa noite!

Good night!

livro
book

travesseiro
pillow

Index

About Portuguese

Portuguese is the first language of more than 270 million people around the world. It is the sixth most common language. It is the official language of nine countries on three continents. About 70 percent of Portuguese speakers live in Brazil in South America. There are also millions of Portuguese speakers in Angola and Mozambique in Africa, and Portugal in Europe. Portuguese is also spoken by communities in India, China, and the United States. Many Portuguese words come from the Arabic language.